ON THE EDGE OF SILENCE

A MOUNTAIN ANTHOLOGY

First published 1993
Springbank Press
Helensburgh G84 8XH

This selection copyright
© Springbank Press

ISBN 0 9521976 0 X

Typset by Dittoprint Limited
Printed in Great Britain by
Spectra Print, Glasgow

ON THE EDGE OF SILENCE

A MOUNTAIN ANTHOLOGY

Compiled by
MARY-JANE SELWOOD

With illustrations by
S-J. SELWOOD AND H. FABINI

Introduction by
NIGEL TRANTER

Springbank Press, Helensburgh

CONTENTS

And so from the hills we return refreshed in body, in mind and in spirit. *(F.S. Smythe)*

The secret joy of peril *(Freya Stark)*

INTRODUCTION
by
Nigel Tranter

It is with a sense of commitment and a very real appreciation that I commend this collection of mountain verses and poems, not only to lovers of the hills and open spaces, to climbers of more than mountains but to tacklers of every sort of challenge; also to all who recognise that life here and hereafter is for living to the full, and that achievement, on whatever the scale, is to be measured by the effort and the will rather than the end result.

Like Mark Selwood, Philip Tranter my son, was a dedicated reacher for the heights, and attained to many of them in his twenty-seven years, not least in the peaks of the Hindu Kush, but in numerous other aspects of life. Mark and he set their sights high, and led others to do the same.

The *Mark Selwood Memorial Fund* is a splendid memorial, itself tackling something very demanding and worthwhile. It deserves to be supported. It is a practical celebration of a life, young but very active and full, and though cut short in one aspect, it is only one; probably Mark has found ample further and even more rewarding challenges where he has gone.

Poetry is the distillation of very chosen words to make maximum impact on the imagination and perceptions. This selection indeed speaks for itself. Unto the hills...!

Mark Durham Selwood, to whose memory this book is dedicated, was twenty-seven when he died whilst climbing in the Cairngorms. He loved the mountains passionately and had climbed in Scotland, the European Alps, the Himalayas and New Zealand. Mark was, in Nigel Tranter's words, *"a reacher for the heights"*, not only in the mountains, but more especially in his personal and professional life. Whilst his achievements in all these were great, Mark would probably prefer to be remembered in the words of one of his patients:

> *"He was never too busy to talk or to listen.*
> *In our hearts Dr Selwood's compassion and*
> *kindness will live on for ever."*

The Memorial Fund established in Mark's name seeks to extend this compassion beyond his tragically short life and to help those in need as he would have wished to do. The proceeds from the sale of this book will help to further the medical aid work supported by the *Mark Selwood Memorial Fund*.

For Mark, my son,

MAY the road rise with you,
May the wind be always at your back,
May the sun shine warm upon your face,
And the rains fall soft upon your fields,
And, until we meet again
May God keep you in the hollow of his hand.

Gaelic blessing

The religion of the mountain is in reality
the religion of joy.

J. C. Smuts

MOUNTAINS

To love without conquest
as I you all my days,
love with a zest
as unquenchable as ways
to fulfilment were barred -

is to be lifted and blessed
truly, for what is gained,
soon palls. But that far crest
never touched, never attained
makes of the mind a sky, starred.

Gregory Blunt

LOVE OF MOUNTAINS

If love is
a perfect exchange of souls
my love is a mountain.

If love is
the embrace of unfailing arms
my love is the corrie of a mountain.

If love is
a song under the stars
my love is the mountain of the night.

If love is
tranquil in turmoil
silent in trust
rock in shifting sand
my love is the unfailing mountain.

If love is
eagle-loyal
lichen-tenacious
berry-bright
my love is the living mountain.

If love is
true
if love is
forever
if love is

my love is the eternal mountain.

Jim Crumley

A brilliant sun spangled the snow and the precipices of Ben a'
Bhuird hung bright rose-red above us. How crisp, how bright a
world! but, except for the crunch of our own boots on the
snow, how silent. Once some grouse fled noiselessly away and
we lifted our heads quickly to look for a hunting eagle. And
down valley he came, sailing so low above our heads that we
could see the separate feathers of the pinions against the sky, and
the lovely lift of the wings when he steadied them to soar. Near
the top of the glen there were coal-tits in a tree, and once a
dipper plunged outright into the icy stream. But it was not an
empty world. For everywhere in the snow were the tracks of
birds and animals.

Nan Shepherd, from "The Living Mountain"

I will lift up mine eyes unto the hills,
from whence cometh my help,
My help cometh from the Lord,
which made heaven and earth.

Psalm 121

HURRAHING IN HARVEST

....

And the azurous hung hills are his world-wielding
    shoulder
Majestic - as a stallion stalwart, very-violet-sweet! -
These things, these things were here and but
    the beholder
Wanting; which two when they once meet,
The heart rears wings bold and bolder
And hurls for him, O half hurls earth for him
    off under his feet.

Gerard Manley Hopkins

The Alps seemed to him to be
the folded wings of the earth.

Hans Andersen

I climb'd the roofs at the break of day;
Sun-smitten Alps before me lay.
I stood among the silent statues,
And statued pinnacles, mute as they.

How faintly-flush'd, how phantom-fair,
Was Monte Rosa, hanging there,
A thousand shadowy-pencilled valleys
And snowy dells in a golden air.

Alfred Lord Tennyson

MIST

Rain, do not fall
Nor rob this mist at all,
That is my only cell and abbey wall.

Wind, wait to blow
And let the thick mist grow,
That fills the rose-cup with a whiter glow.

Mist, deepen still
And the low valley fill;
You hide but taller trees, a higher hill.

Still, mist draw close;
These gain by what they lose,
The taller trees and hill, the whiter rose.

All else begone,
And leave me here alone
To tread this mist where earth and sky are one.

Andrew Young

LOCH LOMOND

Mountains open their hinged reflections
    on the loch,
shape and reshape themselves, grow squat
    or tall,
are bent by shakes of light. We never find
the same place twice; which is why picture postcards
that claim to lay the constant on the table
(the camera cannot lie) are popular;
what trotting tourists hoped to purchase for
    the shelf;
the image they'd retain, if they were able.

But landscape's an evasion of itself.

Maurice Lindsay

These great cathedrals of the earth, with their gates of rock, pavements of cloud, choirs of stream and stone, altars of snow, and vaults of purple traversed by continual stars.

John Ruskin

Above them, still enormously above them, earth towered away towards the snowline, where from east to west, across hundreds of miles, ruled as with a ruler, the last of the bold birches stopped. Above that, in scarps and blocks upheaved, the rocks strove to fight their heads above the white smother. Above these again, changeless since the world's beginning, but changing to every mood of sun and cloud, lay out the eternal snow.

Rudyard Kipling, from 'Kim'

...Suddenly I came out of the mist and into dazzling sunshine. I found myself on a narrow ridge of virgin snow which thrust above the cloud, and only 100 feet higher the graceful summit stood gleaming against the blue of the sky... At 11.30 we had made it. We were perched on the roof of the world, 20,000 feet high, where no man had ever stood before. The Hindu Kush was shrouded in mist beneath our feet.

Philip Tranter, from "No Tigers in the Hindu Kush"

The bold profile silhouettes the skyline,
strong and upright.
The crevasses jagged and steep,
drop into the dense crags.

The surrounding air is cool,
the atmosphere intense.
Right at the summit,
it's a different world.

On the glacier, open and free,
I stand glancing around,
taking in the views and air,
I am alone, at peace, in freedom.

Rowan Hamilton (Age 13)

On top of a mountain,
On top of the world,
So lonely,
Way up high.

Douglas Easton (Age 10)

Mountains so high to the deep blue sky
Singing for fun under the sun
Until
Slowly the mist
Spreads over the sky.
You can't see the tops ever so high.
Mountains I love
Mountains are free.
I think the mountains are singing to me.

Jennifer Hamill (Age 8)

As I look at a mountain,
towering in the sky.
I think it is like a fountain,
I really don't know why.

Maybe because it's tall,
sprouting from the land.
Even though it's small,
from where I stand.

When you see a mountain,
it appears really grand.
But, I can cover it,
behind one hand.

Matthew Smith (Age 10)

MOUNTAIN

The draped valleys
Hung from summits.
The sharpened pinnacles
Rising higher.
The beauty....
... of nature.

Lovat Hamilton (Age 10)

Just one breath,
and I wonder
why?
Just one glance,
and I have found
my answer.

Lovat Hamilton (Age 10)

HILL ROLLING

I kind of exploded inside,
And joy shot out of me.
I began my roll down the grassy hill.
I bent my knees up small, took a deep breath
    and I was off.
My arms shot out sideways.
I gathered speed.
My eyes squinted.
Sky and grass, dazzle and dark.

I went on forever,
My arms were covered with dents,
    holes, squashed grass.
Before I knew it, I was at the bottom.
The game was over.
The door of the classroom closed behind me.
I can smell chalk dust, and hear the voice
    of the teacher,
to make me forget my hill.

Andrew Taylor

Mountains of Yoshino
Shedding petals,
swallowing clouds.

Buson

The song of mountain streams unheard by day,
Now hardly heard, beguiles my homeward way.
All air is, as the sleeping water, still,
Listening the aerial music of the hill.

William Wordsworth

I believe that I now understand in some small measure why the Buddhist goes on pilgrimage to a mountain. The journey is itself part of the technique by which the god is sought. It is a journey into Being; for as I penetrate more deeply into the mountain's life, I penetrate also into my own. For an hour I am beyond desire. It is not ecstasy, that leap out of the self that makes man like a god. I am not out of myself, but in myself. I am. To know Being, this is the final grace accorded from the mountain.

Nan Shepherd, from "The Living Mountain"

Just go on and on.... Do you see the mountain ranges there, far away? One behind another, they rise up. They tower. That is my deep, unending, inexhaustible kingdom.

Henrik Ibsen, from "The Master Builder"

The mountain keeps silent omni-presiding

Tessa Ransford

HOW SMALL IS MAN

Why climb the mountains? I will tell you why,
And if my fancy jumps not with your whim,
What marvel? there is scope beneath the sky
For things that creep, and fly, and walk, and swim.
I love the free breath of the broad-winged breeze.
I love the eye's free sweep from craggy rim,
I love the free bird poised at lofty ease,
And the free torrent's far up-sounding hymn;
I love to leave my littleness behind
In the low vale where little cares are great,
And in the mighty map of things to find
A sober measure of my scanty state,
Taught by the vastness of God's pictured plan
In the big world how small a thing is man!

John Stuart Blackie

UP THERE

I know that it is today, and that there was yesterday,
and will be tomorrow;
But up there, where the hills are deep in snow,
    that is eternity:
That is out of all reckoning and telling.
You can't measure that proud white beauty,
But you can live with it for a little space,
That will not belong to today, or yesterday, or tomorrow,
But to the time beyond time.

Margaret Cropper

All littleness was gone from the mountain now. His world was one with the elements, the sky, great stars and gigantic crags: silent except when now and then came a roar from something breaking in the glacier or the thunder of a boulder falling.

John Masefield, from "Sard Harker"

Among the peaks under the spell of his rhythmical bodily movements, he and the silent mountains stand face to face as pure living sensation and lifeless matter; and each finds in the other a mysterious completion.

N. Trevenen Huxley

The mountain keeps silent
omni-presiding
and wise trees wait wordless,

Words heap unuttered
crumpled inside me.

Tessa Ransford, from "Shadows from the Greater Hill"

POEM FOR A DEPARTING MOUNTAINEER

Regarding the skyline longingly
(curved as a body, my own, I desire you)
where ink-coloured cloud masses
and rolls on the ridge,
I pick out silhouettes. Deer
dolmen, trees, perhaps tombs
raised through the bracken and weird
midsummer nights by the ancients.
Or men. I can't discern, and mustn't wonder
whether the figures are vibrant, stone,
setting out hunched under loads
or turning home. I must be distant,
draw the curtains for bed,
and leave them, like you who left
with your grave-goods strapped to your back
alone to the lowering cloud.

Kathleen Jamie

EXCLUDED BY MOUNTAINS

We have always believed in mountains,
their inwardness, and how they ascend
to perimeters of blue; high lords they are.

Their heads are always turned away,
their thoughts ruthless. Consider the essence
of stone, how men dying of thirst

will suck a pebble yet still go mad,
their senses unweighted. Reflect how the prophet
on finding truths as certain as flint
discovers them more obdurate than his own despair.
And how little the hand achieves on squeezing,
hard, even smallest grit, and bleeds on separation.

So do not expect, but extend your arm, touch
with most careful fingertips this huge rock,
and feel the cold surface of a great god's back.

Norman Kreitman

The Mountains - grow unnoticed -
Their Purple figures rise
Without attempt - Exhaustion -
Assistance - or Applause -

In Their Eternal Faces
The Sun - with just delight
Looks long - and last - and golden -
for fellowship - at night -

Emily Dickinson

The sea beckons
Again and again
to the mountains. Unmoved
the austere mountains ponder
a silence as profound as stars.

Hone Tuwhare

MOUNTAIN

By billions the days turned
When lightning varicosed the air
And the ground vomited and spat
In the rain's grey percussion,
In the sun's red silence.

The dithering sea ebbed
And pleats of stranded earth
Rose groan by long groan;
A vast block rearing
In stealth like a dinosaur
From the land's split egg,
Carrying in its dark flesh
Shells kilned and secret
Far, far and forever lifted
To the beach of the sky.

Flocked seasons came and flew
While below wind below wing
Water sucked stone to runnels
And ice, plucking black scabs
From the rock's skin, helped
The weather saw its spine to crags
Where the trees' sheet could not reach.

Then we - newfangled, overawed -
Struggled upright stammering
Mountain.

Catriona Malan

HIGH UP ON SUILVEN

Gulfs of blue air, two lochs like spectacles,
A frog (this height) and Harris in the sky -
There are more reasons for hills
Than being steep and reaching only high.

Meeting the cliff face, the American wind
Stands up on end: chute going the wrong way.
Nine ravens play with it and
Go up and down its lift half the long day.

Reasons for them? The hill's one...A web like this
Has a thread that goes beyond the possible;
The old spider outside space
Runs down it - and where's raven? Or where's hill?

Norman MacCaig

THE MOUNTAIN IN SPRING

All that survived is convalescent now,
Content to live.
The mountain rears above, inscrutable,
And from its bony shoulders and its brow
The distant streams
Hang like pale ribbons. On its sparse-clad ribs
Sheep, tired, with trailing fleeces, seek their lambs.
Below, the valley stretches like a cat,
Lazy and striped and warm and full of dreams.
The bent trees stir. The ragged birds respond
With a thin sweetness, forgetful of their dead.
Far down, upon the coloured stamp-like fields
The farm is but a toy,
A sugar-cube, white as remembered snow.
Lean cows are creeping dots of cream and red -
And man too small to see.

The mountain rears above, inflexible.
The mountain, stern, unmoved by death or life,
Or grief or joy,
Had done with pain these million years ago.

Phyllis Lyth

NANT-Y-CERDDIN

In high morning I am haunted
   by long-ago mornings -
and even those were ghost-ridden
   by a more distant morning
never quite remembered
   but never dying at noon.
Today when wheatears
   flash from sunny rocks
And new loose-limbed lambs
stagger appalled through the stony stream
   after stolid ewes;
when daffodils blow in the nettle-garden
   of a farm with broken windows,
and in a remote brown valley
the clammy standing stone
   grows warm to touch -
even today ghosts come
   whispering of a ghost.
Could there ever be a morning unhaunted,
a spring shining
   with no sunlight but its own?
Only the first perhaps,
   the lost ideal morning,
the one that must be found,
must be lived or haunt me always,
the lost morning on forgotten hills.

Ruth Bidgood

HOKUSAI

The wave lifts, curls
Will break, scattering foam;

The petals will blow from these flowers,
Already the wind stirs
And here come the hurrying horsemen
Ducking their heads for speed,

Look - the moment is gone,
Look - where the leaves fly,

Sunset again at the end of the street
Scatters clouds in different directions

And there, you say, is the lake with the
        unruffled surface,
There is the eternal calm horizon line
And Mount Fuji, turning only
Through all the stages of incandescence
And back to ashen blue, burning
Yet never burned.

You lived with a mountain
There at the bottom of your street
Making it easier perhaps
Not to be temporarily blinded
By the storms of leaves, petals, tears?

Rosalind Brackenbury

OF HIGH SOLITUDE

Eagles and isles and uncompanioned peaks,
The self-reliant isolated things
Release my soul, embrangled in the stress
Of all day's crass and cluttered business;
Release my soul in song, and give it wings;
And even when the traffic roars and rings,
With senses stunned and beaten deaf and blind,
My soul withdraws into itself, and seeks
The peaks and isles and eagles of the mind.

Wilfred W. Gibson

closer, closer
to paradise -
how cold.

Issa

May be it's only in
your prison
with bars of ice
enclosing you around
that you can turn
inside and find
that melody,
that shining song and
hear it sound.

Jehanne Mehta

THE SUMMIT

Farther than I have been
All is changed: no water for moist souls,
Wind and stone is the world of the summit,
    stone and rain,
Stone, wind and cold, only the oldest things remain,
And wind unceasing has blown,
Without beginning or ending the wind has blown.

Noise of wind on rock cries to the soul 'Away,
Away, what wilt thou do?' The butterfly
Blown up against the summit meets the snow,
Those who rise there endure
Dragon of stone and dragon of air; by wind
    irresistible
Hurled, or still as stone, the long way
A dream while the wing of a bird
Brushes a grain of quartz from the unmoved hill.

Kathleen Raine, from "Bheinn Naomh"

And so from the hills we return refreshed in body,
in mind and in spirit.

F. S. Smythe

CLIMBING THE MOUNTAIN

The ridge my eye holds to
Sharp in the sky
Twenty yards ahead
Is never the summit.
It is always further.
So I heave myself on
With boosted will -
Forward to the summit.
The level step
There! The buzzard maybe,
And the scarce primula!
Then the completer view:
Walls I could not see beyond
Walking below
Shall be a net of shadows
A prisoner may walk across.
The main street, haughty,
With honours glittering,
When seen from the peak
Shall be reduced to the ranks
Of highways working
In the unfolded plan
Of pasture, ploughland, rivers, hills.
Ah, the view from the peak -
But the ridge my eyes hold to
Sharp in the sky
Twenty yards ahead
Is never the summit.
It is always further.
So I go on
With boosted will -
Forward to the summit,
For it is the way of a man
Half blinded by land
To be healed by horizons.

Clifford Dyment

...And so from the hills we return refreshed in body, in mind and in spirit, to grapple anew with life's problems. For a while we have lived simply, wisely and happily; we have made good friends; we have adventured well. The hills have taught us to be content in our faith and in the love of God who created them.

F.S. Smythe, from "The Spirit of the Hills"

UNDER THE MOUNTAIN

Seen from above
The foam in the curving bay is a goose-quill
That feathers... unfeathers... itself.

Seen from above
The field is a flap and the haycocks buttons
To keep it flush with the earth.

Seen from above
The house is a silent gadget whose purpose
Was long since obsolete.

But when you get down
The breakers are cold scum and the wrack
Sizzles with stinking life.

When you get down
The field is a failed or a worth-while crop, the source
Of back-ache if not heart-ache.

And when you get down
The house is a maelstrom of loves and hates where you -
Having got down - belong.

Louis MacNeice

COME BY THE HILLS

Come by the hills, to the land where fancy is free
And stand where the peaks meet the sky and the lochs meet the
sea,
Where the rivers run clear and the bracken is gold in the sun,
And the cares of tomorrow can wait till this day is done.

Scottish Folksong

HAVING CLIMBED THE TOPMOST PEAK OF THE INCENSE-BURNER MOUNTAIN

Up and up, the Incense-Burner Peak!
In my heart is stored what my eyes and ears perceived.
All the year - detained by official business;
Today, at last, I got a chance to go.
Grasping the creepers, I clung to dangerous rocks;
My hands and feet - weary with groping for hold.
There came with me three or four friends,
But two friends dared not go further.
At last we reached the topmost crest of the Peak;
My eyes were blinded, my soul rocked and reeled.
The chasm beneath me - ten thousand feet;
The ground I stood on, only a foot wide.
If you have not exhausted the scope of seeing and hearing
How can you realise the wideness of the world?
The waters of the river looked narrow as a ribbon,
P'en Castle smaller than a man's fist.
How it clings, the dust of the world's halter!
It chokes my limbs; I cannot shake it away.
Thinking of retirement, I heaved an envious sigh;
Then, with lowered head, came back to the Ant's Nest.

Po Chu-i (A.D. 819)
(Translated by *Arthur Waley*)

I'll walk where my own nature would be leading,
It vexes me to choose another guide;
Where the grey flocks in ferny glens are feeding,
Where the wild wind blows on the mountain side.

What have these lonely mountains worth revealing?
More glory and more grief than I can tell;
The earth that wakes one human heart to feeling
Can centre both the worlds of Heaven and Hell.

Emily Bronte

CLIMBING THE HILL WITHIN THE DEAFENING WIND

Climbing the hill within the deafening wind
The blood unfurled itself, was proudly borne
High over meadows where white horses stood;
Up the steep woods it echoed like a horn
Till at the summit under shining trees
It cried: Submission is the only good;
Let me become an instrument sharply stringed
For all things to strike music as they please.

How to recall such music, when the street
Darkens? Among the rain and stone places
I find only an ancient sadness falling,
Only hurrying and troubled faces,
The walking of girls' vulnerable feet,
The heart in its own endless silence kneeling.

Philip Larkin

THE HOMECOMING

Coming down in the snow
From the echoes of a whole day's mountain
The feet sludge, eyes marching
We blunder over streams, swelled by cold
Hands gasping. Too downcast
To see the orange fires of home lights
Singing in a line miles on.
Words are blistered with the dreams of sleep
We have fallen through our own crevasses
Careless and ready to bargain for soft night,
Easy fire, a draught of warm rest
After each scarred step. One thing alone is true
The world ahead has never seemed so good
Its land more true, the gold of windows
Quite so full of light.

Kenneth C. Steven

FROM SKYE, EARLY AUTUMN

I hope that Death is a pass
Through the brown-green, blue-brown, blue-grey,
   grey-ghost mountains,
With the mists hanging in the vales,
   hiding the hard places;
The calm sheep proving my path;
And the sun shining soft
On the loch I have left.

M.L. Michal

UTE MOUNTAIN

'When I am gone,'
the old chief said,
'if you need me, call me,'
and down he lay, became stone.

They were giants then
(as you may see),
and we
are not the shadows of such men.

The long splayed Indian hair
spread ravelling out
behind the rocky head
in groins, ravines;

petered across the desert plain
through Colorado,
transmitting force
in a single, undulant, unbroken line

from toe to hair-tip: there
profiled, inclined away from one
are features, foreshortened, and the high
blade of the cheekbone.

Reading it so, the eye
can take the entire great
straddle of mountain-mass,
passing down elbows, knees and feet.

'If you need me, call me.'
His singularity dominates the plain
as we call to our aid his image:
thus men make a mountain.

Charles Tomlinson

VIEWPOINT

*Why can't they give these damn mountains
proper names?* Their names are
in our language. The mountains
understand it and know each other
by these proper Gaelic names.

*Why can't they be spelt so we can
pronounce them? - like Ben Nevis
or Ring of Bright Water?*
The spelling is the way it works
and makes everything real.

*I can't remember these names.
What does 'Sgurr' mean?*
Steep, high, impenetrable peak
that divides our minds, our speech
and our understanding.

Here's one I can say: Ben Tee.
And here is Gleouraich, Gairich,
Spidean Mialach, Sgurr na Ciche.

(Mist and clouds are swirling
as an eagle soars and falls.)

*What is that range called, that
you see and then it fades?*
Knoydart. It means 'Rough Bounds!'
Dear, far, near, fearsome
rough bounds of our being.

Tessa Ransford

LOOSED COLD

Still, still
the mountains rise behind
red-blue in the gray
the cold is loosed
has waved itself off from the landscape
which now lies softening.

Guðrið Helmsdal

A MESSY MAN'S MOUNTAINS THESE

A messy man's mountains these,
Like the maker knew no extremes
and only that -
No in-betweens.
Steep and more than steep
And shaped the way a child might
    draw a mountain.

Couldn't help but see
the foothills as left-overs,
Spill-over from above.
Left roughly rounded
and looking like good foothills should.

And waterfalls!
Not just one or two
But hundreds scarring the view.

Today in the rain
I caught a glimpse of Aspiring
Rock and water perfect.

Kim Dawson

MOUNTAINS AT NIGHT

The lake has died down,
The reed, black in its sleep,
Whispers in a dream.
Expanding immensely into the
    countryside,
The mountains loom outspread.
They are not resting.
They breathe deeply, and hold
    themselves,
Pressed tightly to one another.
Deeply breathing,
Laden with mute forces,
Caught in a wasting passion.

Hermann Hesse
(Translated by *James Wright*)

Moon golden towards the full,
Summits of pine afloat
Over level mist, the hills
Cloudlike, adrift.

Kathleen Raine

THE GREEN LAKE

Eloquent are the hills: their power speaks
In ice, rock and falling stone;
The voices of croziered fern, wood-sorrel, gentian, edelweiss,
Lead upward to the summit or the high col.

The mountain lake mirrors the hills, and the white clouds
Move in a blue depth, the hut stands empty;
No one appears all day, nothing disturbs
The symphony of ice and yellow rock and the blue shadow.

And at dusk the familiar sequence: the light
Lingering on the peak; and near the horizon
Apricot-coloured skies, then purple; and the first stars;
An hour of bustle in the hut, and then silence.

Only at two in the morning men stir in the bunks,
Look out of the windows, put on their boots,
Exchange a word with the guardian, curse the cold,
And move with a force beyond their own to the high peaks.

Be still for once. Do not sing,
Let the blood beat its symphony unanswered;
Remain here by the lake for a whole day
With the sky clear and the rocks asking to be climbed.

There is music in movement, in the song, the dance,
The swing of the accordion in the crowded hut,
The swing of the axe in the icefall; but be still.
Listen. There is another voice that speaks.

Michael Roberts

CLIMBING THE RIDGE

A little while, to climb the ridge again:
The body flowing, smooth, on reels of silk;
Wicks of cotton-grass in winter sun
Luminous; red moss; the soil's black butter
Salted with white sand.
      A little while
To see through wind-gapped mist the fields below
Gleam like ocean shoals, the lake a spearhead
Barbed and tanged with light.
      A little while
To lie back under white sky; hooded, sleep;
Wake from warm throb to the kiss of snow
And come down-mountain, careless, like a rock-fall.
To say: where does it go?

Beyond the edge of hearing curlews cry.
The pools, wind-shivered, wait for others now.
What is there here to mourn?

Your song is in the silence.
Your stone is on the cairn.

David Sutton

CHILTERN

I do not like
harmless hills
they are cautious
freeing sides
to Welsh wind

winter
knows how
to waylay
a landscape
with strangeness

knows how
to recall
a hill
from oblivion

winter allows
cloud
to come between
gods and prey.

David J. Morley

The secret joy of peril

Freya Stark

Climbing is a way of studying the Ultimate Unknown. In the curious playgrounds of their sport, mountaineers learn what primitive peoples know instinctively - that mountains are the abode of the dead, and that to travel into the high country is not simply to risk death but to risk understanding it.

Robert Leonard Reid, from "The Great Blue Dream"

THE CRAGSMAN

In this short span
between my finger-tips on the smooth edge
and these tense feet cramped to the crystal ledge
I hold the life of man.
Consciously I embrace
arched from the mountain rock on which I stand
to the firm limit of my lifted hand
the front of time and space:-
    For what is there in all the world for me
    but what I know and see?
    And what remains of all I see and know,
    if I let go?

With this full breath
bracing my sinews as I upward move
boldly reliant to the rift above
I measure life from death.
With each strong thrust
I feel all motion and all vital force
borne on my strength and hazarding their course
in my self-trust:-
    There is no movement of what kind it be
    but has its source in me;
    and should these muscles falter to release
    motion itself must cease.

In these two eyes
that search the splendour of the earth, and seek
the sombre mysteries on plain and peak,
all vision wakes and dies.

With these my ears
that listen for the sound of lakes asleep
and love the larger rumour from the deep,
the eternal hears:-
    For all of beauty that this life can give
    lives only while I live;
    and with the light my hurried vision lends
    all beauty ends.

Geoffrey Winthrop Young

EVEREST

Reason is silenced here: she cannot speak
For them who dare the Himalayan peak:
It is the venture, even in mischance,
Which claims that man surmounts his circumstance.

William Soutar

THE RUNE AND THE ECHO

The Climbers

    'Now and tomorrow
    O hill-gods grant us
    the breadth of your vision,
    the calm of your vapours -
    granite's stability,
    heather's tenacity,
    cataract's purity,
    poise of your pinnacles
    reaching to heaven.'

The Echo

    'Now and forever
    our ways be unto you
    challenge and conquest
    stern and sufficing -
    white peace of our snows,
    grey grief of our rains,
    flame of our sunsets,
    freedom of eagles -
    a dream in our dust.'

Brenda Macrow

And now the mountains would not let him rest,
Even from childhood they had seemed to him
Presences towering over daily life.
He had grown familiar as his boy's strength waxed,
With every track and climb and rocky summit;
But not familiar with the mountain's self,
So grave, austere and inaccessible,
Now come to judgement with his faltering spirit.

Margaret Cropper

ALTARS OF ROCK

What have you seen on the summits, the peaks
    that plunge their
Icy heads into space? What draws you trembling
To blind altars of rock where man cannot linger
Even in death, where body grows light, and vision
Ranging those uninhabitable stations
Dazzled and emulous among the rage of summoning
Shadows and clouds, may lead you in an instant
Out from all footing? What thread of music,
    what word in
That frozen silence that drowns the noise of
    our living?

Charles Brasch

HAROLD'S LEAP

Harold, are you asleep?
Harold, I remember your leap,
It may have killed you
But it was a brave thing to do.
Two promontories ran high into the sky,
He leapt from one rock to the other
And fell to the sea's smother.
Harold was always afraid to climb high,
But something urged him on,
He felt he should try.
I would not say that he was wrong,
Although he succeeded in doing nothing but die.
Would you?
Ever after that steep
Place was called Harold's Leap.
It was a brave thing to do.

Stevie Smith

Change was his mistress, Chance his councillor,
Love could not hold him, Duty forged no chain;
The wide seas and the mountains called to him,
And grey dawns saw his camp-fire in the rain.

Anon

IN THE SHADOW OF THE MOUNTAIN

In the shadow of the mountain
there lived a boy of a restless age.
Neither time nor people could hold him,
Always moving to another phase.

In the shadow of the mountain
he found bits of love but couldn't stay;
a home or promises couldn't keep him,
nor things that people to him would say.

In the shadow of the mountain
he built his life near the river's bend;
lived each day in hope and searching.
Never sure his searching would ever end.

In the shadow of the mountain
he controlled his patience night and day
but soon his restlessness would find him.
Then, one early morning, he drifted away

In the shadow of the mountain
as the buds of spring appear.
Those who knew him hold the memory
of his dreams, held in a lonely sphere,

Of a boy who touched the sunlight
cradled love within his hands
wanting only to love people
in his vast enchanted land.

Walter Rinder

As o'er the mountains walks the wandering soul,
Seeking for rest, in his unresting spirit...

Anon (c.1600)

....The secret joy of peril comes from the veiled presence, without which most savour goes; and this is no morbid feeling, for the ecstasy belongs not to death in itself, but to *life*, suddenly enriched to know itself alive. So, after a summer dawn and climb till noon, among clefts and icy triangles or wind-scooped crannies, the mountaineer returning sets foot again on the short turf and flowers; and the breeze that cools him is the same breeze that sways the harebells; the blood that tramples in his ears and runs like chariots through his veins is the kind, swift, temporary stuff by which the smaller things of earth are fed; he is back in the community of his kind and descends light-footed, among the pastures: but he remembers how in the high silences he has known himself on the edge of Silence and how its wing has brushed him.

Freya Stark, from "Perseus in the Wind"

HAIKU

Alone I cling to
  The freezing mountain and see
    White cloud - below me.

Ian Serraillier

But it is of the nature of mysteries that they cannot be
interpreted to those who do not know. To the unbeliever, they
sound like mockeries, or, at best, the unmeaning fancies of an
idle singer of an empty day... Let those who are indifferent to
mountains protest in the name of sanity and common sense.
Perhaps the climber is to be envied his good fortune in being
something more than sane.

Hugh Rose Pope

ACKNOWLEDGEMENTS

The editor would like to acknowledge the generosity of many friends who gave their time, help and advice to further this project, in particular, Campbell Brown and Steven Wiggins of B & W Publishing, Michael Downie of Dittoprint, Tessa Ransford from the Scottish Poetry Library and Sheona McLennan for her help with the cover design. To her close friends and long-suffering husband and children she would like to say thank you for their unfailing support, patience and understanding.

The editor and publishers are grateful to all authors, agents and publishers who have kindly given permission to print copyright material and would like to make the following acknowledgements:

Jim Crumley for "Love of Mountains".

National Trust for Scotland for two excerpts from "The Living Mountain" by Nan Shepherd.

The Andrew Young Estate for "Mist" by Andrew Young.

The Mercat Press, Edinburgh, "Collected Poems 1940-1990" for "Loch Lomond" by Maurice Lindsay.

Nigel Tranter and Hodder and Stoughton for an excerpt from "No Tigers in the Hindu Kush" by Nigel Tranter.

The Penguin Group and Lucien Styk for poems by Buson and Issa.

Tessa Ransford for "Viewpoint" and an excerpt from "Shadows from the Greater Hill".

Kathleen Jamie for "Poem for a departing mountaineer", reprinted by permission of Bloodaxe Books Ltd from "The Way We Live" by Kathleen Jamie (Bloodaxe Books, 1987).

Norman Kreitman for "Excluded by Mountains".

The Canterbury Mountaineering Club, New Zealand for "The sea beckons" by Hone Tuwhare and "A Messy Man's Mountains These" by Kim Dawson.

Catriona Malan for "Mountain".

Norman MacCaig and Random House UK Limited for "High up on Suilven".

Ruth Bidgood and Poetry Wales Press Ltd for"Nant-y-Cerddin".

Rosalind Brackenbury for "Hokusai".

Phyllis Lyth and "The Countryman" who originally published "The Mountain in Spring".

Macmillan London Ltd for "Of High Solitude" by Wilfred Gibson.

Jehanne Mehta for an excerpt from her song "December", recorded on cassette "Green Jack II 1983".

Kathleen Raine for "The Summit" from "Bheinn Naomh" and "Moon golden towards the full".

Sheil Land Associates Ltd acting on behalf of the Estate of F.S. Smythe for an excerpt from "The Spirit of the Hills" by F.S. Smythe, published by Hodder and Stoughton 1935.

Miss Irene Dyment for "Climbing the Mountain" by Clifford Dyment.

Faber & Faber Ltd for "Under the Mountain" by Louis MacNeice from "Collected Poems 1925-1948", published 1949.

George Allen & Unwin, now Unwin Hyman, an imprint of Harper Collins Publishers Limited, for the poem by Po Chu-i, translated by Arthur Waley.

Faber & Faber Ltd for "Climbing the hill within the deafening wind" by Philip Larkin from "Collected Poems" first published 1988.

Kenneth C. Steven for "Homecoming".

M.L. Michal and "The Countryman" who first published "From Skye, Early Autumn".

Oxford University Press and Professor Tomlinson for "Ute Mountain" from "American Scenes".

Wilfion Books and Gudrid Helmsdal for "Loosed Cold", from "Rocky Shores", an anthology of Faroese Poetry.

Faber & Faber Ltd for "The Green Lake" by Michael Roberts from "Orion Marches".

David Sutton and Peterloo Poets for "Climbing the Ridge" from Settlements", available at £5.95 from Peterloo Poets, 2 Kelly Gardens, Calstock, Cornwall.

Random House UK Limited for the excerpt from "The Great Blue Dream" by Robert Leonard Reid.

Miss Brenda Macrow and Oliver & Boyd Ltd, Edinburgh for "The Rune and the Echo" by Brenda Macrow.

Alan Roddick, literary executor, for Charles Brasch's "Altars of Rock".

Virago for "Harold's Leap" by Stevie Smith, copyright James McGibbon,1937,1938,1942,1950,1957, 1962,1966,1971,1972,1981.

"In the Shadow of the Mountain" excerpted from "The World I Used to Know" by Walter Rinder. Reprinted by permission of Celestial Arts, P.O.Box 7327, Berkeley CA 94707.

John Murray (publishers) Ltd for the excerpt from "Perseus in the Wind" by Freya Stark.

"Haiku" by Ian Serraillier from "I'll Tell You a Tale" copyright (c) Ian Serraillier, 1973, 1976. Published in Puffin Books. Reprinted by permission of Penguin Books Ltd.

The High School of Glasgow, Junior School, and Lomond School, Helensburgh, for contributions by children.

Sarah-Jane Selwood and Helmut Fabini for exclusive rights to reproduce original art work in this publication.

Every effort has been made to secure permission to reprint the poems and excerpts in this anthology. Where it has not been possible to trace sources for copyright material the editor and publishers apologise and would be glad to be notified of any additions or corrections.